Coffee,

Alcohol, and

Heartbreak

A Poetry Collection

T.B. Wittkofsky

CONTENTS

Acknowledgements

THESE POEMS REPRESENT SOME of my darkest times. I want to start by thanking everyone wo inspired these poems, whether for better or worse. Even though some of my inspirations hurt me in some way or another, I was able to turn that pain into something beautiful, something that I could use to help people.

I want to thank MaMa for all she has done to inspire my writing. Ever since I was little, she encouraged me to write and pushed me to do better in everything I did. Her constant reminder that I am capable of whatever I set my mind to has helped lead me to where I am today.

Next, I want to thank Mrs. Sandra Shuford. A teacher I had in elementary school, she turned out to be one of my biggest inspirations and perhaps one of my biggest fans. The lessons she taught me and the kindness in her heart inspire me every day.

Finally, I must thank my fiancé Gracie. She has been the driving force in my life since I met her, always pushing me to do more. She challenges me to be a better person and helps me reach my goals. I can read her every page of my writing and she will listen to every word.

There are so many more people in my life that I can thank, Mom, Grandy, Justin, Belle and Dutch just to name a few. But in the form of this poetry, the four aforementioned inspirations required special attention.

Thank you for taking the time to read my poetry, never forget that you are not alone.

MY RAINBOW

WAIT FOR ME ON the other end,
   of this beautiful rainbow,
   going up is always harder than going down the bend.
   i'll come as fast as i can to meet you down below.

   if you look at it the right way,
   it's just our smile upside down,
   as together in the grass we lay,
   looking at the rainbow, making not a sound.

   the vibrant colors our love,
   showing all aspects of our personalities,
   in the sky up above,
   and we don't care who sees.

   we'll dance across the top,
   making it across together,

and holding hands as we drop,
into forever.

first comes the rain,
the stormy days pour upon us,
as we feel the dreaded pain.
we won't go down without a fuss.

then the sun comes out,
drying out the dampness,
baby, don't pout.
we're out of the darkness.

the rain disappears soon.
the sun shines brighter.
our smiles boom.
our love tighter.

then the rainbow appears.
symbolizing our love,
after the hardship of the years,
we've been chosen to be together from up above

THE ULTIMATE CHOICE

HAPPINESS IS A CHOICE,
one that we must make.
we must shout, let the world hear our voice.
remember, it's about what you take.

the littlest things in life,
often make the biggest impact.
we must avoid death's swinging scythe.
land on our feet like a nimble cat.

everyone struggles to get through the day,
a smile can brighten a world.
the kindest words are the best to say.
a smile is the best way to be curled

why bring everyone down?
when you can bring everyone up?
life isn't as pretty when you're looking at it with a frown,
a simple change can be so abrupt

there will always be good,
there will always be bad.
make sure the good shines brighter than the sun could.
brighter than a knight in armor clad.

stand taller than a mighty oak,
stretch your arms wide,
your mighty spirit shan't be broke.
you are the only you, truly bonafide.

THE LAST
CIGARETTE

I INHALE ONE LAST puff of smoke,
   knowing i'm slowly killing myself,
   nothing but remorse for the words i've spoke.
   the only way out is my diminishing health.

   the cigarette burns away,
   much like my life has always been.
   the last ash hanging on by a fray.
   this life, so full of my own sin.

   i just wait for the light to go out,
   the last ember to lose its glow.
   there's nothing left to fight about,
   life's river has begun to slow.

the last ash drops slowly,
drifting towards the ground in slow motion.
reminding me of my life and the point where i got lonely.
the lifelessness caused by this emotion.

as it hits the ground it smolders into oblivion,
draining away all the energy it had left,
bidding the world, a sad end,
while its lungs become compressed.

i draw in a final breath,
but i smile at the finality of it.
for i have nothing left,
and death is my perfect fit.

SIMPLY

DEATH IS A RELEASE.
an escape from an almighty beast.
a time for your troubles to cease,
your simple worries are the least.

death is an escape.
wearing a heroic cape.
showing you what's real and what's fake.
one final awake.

death is relieving,
from all of life's little grieving.
slowly the pain is easing,
slowly you stop breathing...

death is a savior.
cleansing all your terrible behavior,

doing you the best of a favor.
it is life's final gauger.

death is real.
taking forms as sleep or a final meal.
the best and worst of ways to feel.
finding your way to life's seal.

death is desired.
some die, others are admired.
you don't make the decision, you're just fired.
it doesn't matter if you're wide awake or tired.

death is final.
first, last, and primal.
an everlasting cycle,
disrupted by the suicidal.

i'm simply crazy.
lost, confused and hazy.

i'm simply confused.
my mind, too many times, abused.

i'm simply lost.
what has my life cost?

i'm simply frustrated.
losing sight, becoming faded.

i'm simply angry.

COFFEE, ALCOHOL, AND HEARTBREAK

life's disappointed anti.

i'm simply sad.
sick of dealing with all the bad.

i'm simply upset.
every little thing makes me fret.

i'm simply mad.
just wanting things to be different, just a tad.

i'm simply done.
tired of caring for people a ton.

i'm simply fucked up.
tired of caring, no longer giving a fuck.

i'm simply crazy,
the world can no longer phase me.

JUST SMILE

IT'S SO MUCH EASIER to smile,
   when your heart is trapped in a vial.
   knowing the things you did we're so vile.
   just wanting it to last just a little while.

   i can say i'm okay,
   it's simple to say.
   not so simple to obey.
   but in my pain i lay.

   i can pretend everything's alright.
   hold back my words, my tongue i bite.
   eventually though, i'll lose sight.
   i'll lose my will to fight.

   i can tell you i'm not hurt,
   try to turn you from sadness and convert.

you don't need to know how close i am to being under dirt.
i just smile at death when we flirt.

i'm sorry i must lie to you.
but if you only knew...
how far i went, how long my heart flew.
you'd lie too

black.
yearning to have it all back.
carrying your thoughts and feelings in a hidden sack.
pain is nothing but a knack.

red.
red means dead.
the one i dread.
the one that reminds me how i bled.
reminds me of the angry words i said.
i left my mind, simply fled.
confused in my head.
fueled by anger, not knowing what they fed.

white.
trying my best to be strong and fight.
trying with all my might.
day slowly slips into night,
losing all that matters, losing sight.
lungs slow and become tight.
i just want things to be right.
not to get away with flight.

blue.
reminds me of your eyes, of you.
makes me miss it too.
i'm just one, we're not two.
depression sets in, but it's not new.
if not me, then who?
i was scared so i flew.

yellow.
happiness.
cheerful.

glee.
not me.

HACK

FUCKED UP IN MY head,
   cut my arms till i bled.
   everything we ever said,
   led me to self-med.

   i'm scared and lost.
   someone else in control, i'm not the boss.
   sleep? no! turn and toss.
   what did my words cost?

   i'm sorry for what i did.
   my adieu, to you, i bid.
   life's boiling over its low lid.
   i avoided this, i simply hid.

   my problems i should face.
   tackle it spray with mace.

sweet and sour emotions i taste.
my life is a waste.

i want it all back.
i don't want to see darkness, no more black.
locked in the back of my minds small shack,
trying to get out, *hack hack hack*!

please forgive me.
this isn't how i wanted it to be.
i wanted to speak- not of i- but of we.
i just simply cannot see.

i'm lost and blind,
i just need to unwind.
i'm looking for something i cannot find.
to you i want to bind.

forgiveness is what i ask,
for this is my final task.
i look back and put myself last.
i look out for you all, in your happiness i shall bask.

this is my cry for help.
someone hear my poor, sad yelp.
i was happy, my heart did melt.
it was real, what i felt.

i miss you.
i hope you do to.
oh, i hope you do.

APART

WE MAY NOT PHYSICALLY be together,
emotionally we are connected.
we'll be in love forever.
my life you've infected.

one day we'll be with each other,
this i can promise you.
you're my one and only lover,
we must remain true.

a thousand 'i love you's aren't enough,
to describe how much you mean.
i know times are tough,
our future together, i have seen.

we'll make it through this, i swear.
just wait for me on the other side,

always know, never forget, how much i care.
it's just a temporary high tide.

forever and always, and even after,
i'll live you till the day i die,
through the tears and the laughter.
bound together by loves strong tie.

SKIES

OUR LOVE SHINES LIKE the sun,
    because i know you're the one,
    we'll fight till it's done.

    infinite amounts of love like the stars,
    more valuable than fancy cars,
    in a tree our love will be carved.

    our love larger than saturn.
    can you see the pattern?
    story of two sides, eastern and western.

    saturn's ring,
    showing what one day i'll bring,
    as i come down the aisle and the people sing.

    so distant, yet so close like the moon.

one day we'll be together, one day soon.
a love straight out the cartoon.

love stretching further than the milky way.
in my arms you'll lay.
soon, just not today.

space is dark,
our love shines like a spark,
i can hear what we'll say, o hark!

drowning in a pool of love,
soaring like a white dove,
high up above.

swimming to eternity,
where we'll spend it together, you and me.
once blind to love, i can now see:

our love is like the tide,
it has its ups and downs like a ride.
but in the end, we're on the same side.

countless waves try to take us under,
roaring down and striking like thunder,
but not once will we blunder.

75 percent of the world is water,
100 percent of my body is love for the youngest daughter.
with our love we can turn salt to freshwater.

the ocean will always be around,
just like our loves silent sound,
together, forever, we are bound.

THE BEST WITHIN

THEY ASK ME WHAT'S wrong,
  i don't know.
  they all sing the same song.
  i can't blame them, they don't know.

  i hate who i am.
  i can't tell you why.
  my life is one big scam,
  happiness nothing but a lie.

  i'm not good enough for myself,
  and i never will be.
  no amount of wealth can cure this health.
  i'm blinded, i can't see.

  i feel useless,
  nothing i do is right.

COFFEE, ALCOHOL, AND HEARTBREAK

i crave death's sweet kiss,
sometimes it's not so far out of sight.

i don't know why i feel this way,
and that makes me even more angry,
i want to know what to say,
it's nothing anybody did but me.

you ask what you did,
nothing at all.
these feelings have always been here, hid.
now i've been pushed and down i fall.

i have a black pit in my chest,
an aching anchor dragging me down.
life facing me with a test.
i take it without a sound.

the physical pain excruciating,
i awake anyway with the pain.
nothing disappears, it's always fading.
how much longer can i be sane?

the emotional pain, taking its toll.
anger, depression, tears, and fists, all battling to come out,
battering a torture ridden soul.
sometimes i want to cry and others i want to shout.

i do not want to be here.
no place in specific,
just life, my only fear.

living makes me more sick.

GOLD

WHAT GOOD IS A heart of gold,
    when the value of gold is so low?
    "it's such a good thing to have!" i'm always told.
    the truth pains me like a stubbed toe.

    this heart of mine, taken for granted.
    all who use it as a renewable resource,
    like it's a gift, to them just handed.
    without worry of its recourse.

    this heart such a burden,
    trying to hold it together.
    a 'gift' given to few men,
    but lighter than a feather.

    what would it be like without this heat?
    a keen happiness in my eye?

the possibilities endless, that's a mere start.
but for now, i just wish to die.

TICKING TIMER

IF I HAD A timer ticking today,
    i'd spend it with all my close ones.
    without a word to say.
    i'd treasure that ticking timer.
    on the mountain or on the bay.
    i'd have no regrets.
    in the spring sun of may,
    that ticking timer winding down,
    and soon in the ground i would lay.
    when that ticking timer ticks no more.

ANGER

HERE IT COMES AGAIN,
   i feel the pain coursing through my chest.
   this is not for the best!
   this place i've already been.

   my heart beat races,
   my body burns like the sun,
   this battle must be won!
   losing sight, confusing faces.

   my breathing increases rapidly,
   i'm losing sight of what matters,
   then my mind shatters!
   i'm losing the battle badly.

   all of a sudden i feel nothing.
   everything just gone.

this is all wrong!
what happened? what is this thing?

i know where i am now...
i've been here many times before,
residing in the darkness of my core!
this place is dark and foul.

now i wait.
when i awake, i won't remember this.
i'll be there holding my fists!
it seems this is my dark fate.

shh now, i heard a sound.
a monster walking through the murky waters,
should i run? no, why bother!
slowly i turn around.

from the darkness comes a silhouette.
the beast towers over me,
his face i can clearly see!
a trick my mind has set.

the beast appears to be myself.
i must decide what to do on a whim.
i know, i must kill him!
but, what happens when you kill yourself?

i stand up to the beast,
he looks at me with a frown,
then he stands down!

i did not have to die, at least.

light begins to replace the dark,
i begin to come back to reality,
what will i see!
hark! i hear a dark dog's dreary bark.

coming to, i see what i have done.
innocence surrounds the air,
but my mind is completely bare!
for, i am the guilty one.

WHO

YOU DON'T GET IT, do you?
   who am i? who!
   of course, i never knew.
   i never do.
   let me tell you my story too.

   lost in thought.
   every last battle i've fought,
   every heart i've sought,
   nothing given nor brought.
   in this darkness i'm caught.

   frustrated and confused.
   right now, you must be amused,
   it was mine- not yours- to lose.
   my existence abused.
   my emotions misused.

pain, my last hope.
holier than the mighty pope.
cleaner cuts than soap.
falling swiftly, sliding down life's slope.
open your eyes! clear the smoke...

i want to be happy,
instead i get sappy,
please wake me up, slap me!
you want to talk, i'm not chatty.
i'm still here. still unhappy.

HERE

WHERE WERE YOU?
   when i was by myself,
   with no one to turn to,
   weary from looking.

   i was here!
   waiting for you!
   i saw your pain and suffering,
   but i was afraid to ask...

   where were you?
   i was sulking alone,
   waiting for someone to care,
   waiting for a kind soul.

   i was here!
   watching you from afar,

but not wanting to play god.
approaching then retreating.

where were you?
when my mind was slipping,
my body was weakening,
my spirit leaving.

i was here!
trying to catch your attention,
but sadly failing every try.
look at me, look at me!

where were you?
i was standing on the edge,
calling your name,
looking for a reason to stay.

i was here!
fighting death for you,
fending him off,
buying you some time.

where were you?
when december neared,
i grew colder waiting,
waiting for someone to keep me warm.

i was here!
following you closely without notice,
approaching your lifeless temple,

only to find it abandoned.

where was i?
you needed me there with you,
growing colder you were,
you left to find the warmth.

you were here!
but i did not see you,
i had blinded myself.
you have joined me in the warmth now.

ALONE

WITH NOTHING LEFT TO live for,
  where are we to go?
  soon i will realize,
  i am alone.

  there is nobody out there.
  winter slowly approaches,
  i can tell.
  i am alone.

  i get colder,
  in body and mind.
  again, i realize,
  i am alone.

  nobody will listen to me,
  they only hear the black dog.

that is all i hear too.
i am alone.

you there!
do you hear my words?
now i realize,
i am alone.

hello my friend,
tell me; you carry a scythe, are you a farmer?
i see you there, but...
i am alone.

it must be late at night,
you are dressed in a dark robe.
i have realized,
i am alone.

you must be a monk!
with a hood draped over your head.
maybe you hide your face,
i am alone.

you're white as a skeleton friend,
dark pits in your eyes.
looking into them makes me feel empty.
i am alone.

do you not speak because you are mute?
or because nobody will listen?
i will my friend,

i am alone.

i recognize you now!
you have come to take me home.
after all, i have realized,
we are all alone.

MY SOUL

MY SOUL, CRUSHED.
    away my smile is brushed.
    my life is rushed,
    when i speak, it is hushed.

    my soul, cast away.
    nobody listens to what i have to say.
    until in the ground my body lay.
    they will listen on that grey day.

    my soul, stolen.
    my heart has become swollen.
    when we die, we become tollan.
    on earth, we are non-existent, much like vulcan.

    my soul, swarmed with lotus.
    trust no one, y tú brutus?

i creep slowly like a tortoise.
my body deteriorating as if infected with asbestos.

my soul, shredded.
i don't know where i am headed.
my mind sheded.
my body netted.

my soul, eaten.
we're all in a race with death, we will all be beaten.
i look forward to our meeting.
when i have been defeaten.

my soul, burned.
upside down my life becomes turned.
all my life i am spurned.
the space between death and i increases kenned.

my soul, gone.
life is twisted like a python.
colored with a crayon,
by the ones we consider an icon.

my soul, comes to an end.
our ashes blown away with the wind.
no one remembers, not even our kin.
that's when our life truly comes to a fin.

DRIP, DROP

DRIP, DROP, DRIP, DROP.
the crimson tears fall from atop.
representing my pain and sorrow,
other's happiness i've always had to borrow.

drip, drop, drip, drop.
the tears hit the floor with a *plop*.
the pain is like a temporary high,
in this world built on a lie.

drip, drop, drip, drop.
the tears turn into raindrops.
i feel my mind slowly slipping,
as i hear the rain dripping.

drip, drop, drip, drop.
i change the pattern, bottom to top.

i'm going back home,
no longer on this earth shall i roam.

drip, drop, drip, drop.
the tears flow to the ground, sloshing like a wet mop.
my poor baby.
why have you left my heart so achy?
you had so much to live for,
you were so golden down to the core.
my poor baby.
you lift my vision blurry.
why did you leave your poor mother?
i loved you like no other.

my poor baby.
i feel so guilty.
where was i when you needed help?
i did not even hear your sad yelp.
my poor baby.
could i have saved you? just maybe...
you had so many who loved you.
you did not even bid me adieu.

my poor baby.
i'm getting dizzy.
you took your own life,
you beat death and took his scythe.

my poor baby.
i miss you madly.

FREE

I WANT TO BE free.
    free of this pain.
    free of this misery.
    free of the black pit in my chest.
    i can't tell you why i feel this way.
    i can't even tell you how i feel.
    simply because, i don't even know.
    i just know it hurts.
    that sickening pain.
    the pain in your chest.
    you feel sick.
    feel like your heart is expanding.
    crushing your lungs.
    causing you to gasp for air.
    pressing against your chest.
    begging to get out.
    begging to get away from this feeling.

this unexplainable feeling.
the blackness in your chest.
i close my eyes.
all i see is darkness.
that's all there is.
darkness.
nobody there.
nothing to live for.
an empty life.
no purpose.
i want a way out.
but i'm too scared to kill myself.
too scared to run a blade through my arms.
i'm good for nothing.
i can't even kill myself.
so i light a cigarette.
drink another beer.
inhale the smoke into my already crushed lungs.
causing them to push back against my heart.
a struggle in my chest for control.
a pain to escape the pain.
the alcohol flows into my blood stream.
as the blood leaks out, the beer replaces it.
knowing one of the two will kill me.
since i can't do it myself.
i can't even be alone with my own thoughts.
they scare the hell out of me.
i keep my mind busy.
work work work work.
school school school school.

the less time my mind has to think, the less time my heart has to hurt.

i look for someone to fill the void in my mind.to keep me preoccupied.

to keep my thoughts on them, rather than on me.

i just want out.

i want to get away from this place.

not my home.

my life.

i don't want to be here anymore.

i simply can't take it.

i can't be happy.

no matter how hard i try.

i always feel this pain.

my heart constantly expanding.

eventually it'll burst.

eventually it'll push itself away from this pain.

eventually i'll close my eyes for one last time.

whimsically wishing wondrous ways to drift away.

i'll escape this pain.

my heart won't grow anymore.

my lungs won't be crushed.

i won't need alcohol or cigarettes, to feel something besides this pain.

i'll finally have a smile on my face.

the finality of life paints an upside down frown by mistake.

but i'll take a mistaken smile, over none at all.

one will never know the way i feel, much as i'll never know how they feel.

but i'll never wish this pain upon anyone.

because i don't know why i feel this pain.

and they just causes another pain.
and it angers me.
causing another pain.
it makes me upset.
another pain.
i want to kill myself.
more pain.
but i can't, because i'm too scared.
still pain.
cigarettes.
pain.
alcohol.
pain.
life.
pain.

THE COLD

AS THE COLD HITS my skin,
   my memories all begin again.
   remembering what was real,
   remembering what fate has sealed.

   the cool gives rise to tiny bumps,
   reminding me of all my failed triumphs.
   all my failures swarm into my focus,
   clouding my vision like locust.

   the metallic silver glimmering in the moonlight,
   bringing my failures into sight.
   i think this is it,
   my chest swells and is devoured by a dark pit.

   my finger itches to move forward,
   clear my mind of memories stored.

but it freezes mid motion,
stopping myself from life's greatest sin.
was it the cold that froze my action?
or was it the fear of nobody's reaction?
what good what it do,
for death i shall pursue.

what would happen even if i left now?
what difference would it make to the night to
hear a silent, '*pow*'?
the loneliness of afterlife,
is even more freighting than that of life.

the cold falls from my temple,
blood beginning to boil just as simple.
my depression seeps away, replaced with words i want to
say.

once again a failed attempt,
to rid myself of life's cruel intent.
one day i'll be strong,
to beat death for taking so long.

AM I ALIVE?

AM I HERE TODAY?
   do i open my eyes in the morning,
   and close them at night?

   i fight it with all my might,
   but it's hard to win against constant mourning.
   left with nothing to do except pray.

   when talking to god, what do you say?
   all i want to do is know the reason for my scorning.
   this condescending flight.

   all my wrongs in sight,
   not the slightest of warning,
   as the moon gives way to day.

   motionless i still lay,

my mind constantly roaring.
being alone is life's worst plight.

i've laid down my gloves and given up the fight,
as the rain comes pouring,
on this lonesome day in may.

i've given everything away,
my mind is soaring.
my heart beat grows tight.
it only seems right,
that it's the end i'm forging,
but what is this way?

am i cowardly for wanting to get away?
the angels beautifully sing,
as the sky begins to shine bright.

coming into sight,
my eyes adjusting to what they're seeing,
as the angels dance and play.

is this the price to pay,
to experience a feeling greater than my being?
everything goes into the light.

death beautiful burns in white.
no more hurting,
just a beautiful monet.

THUNDER

HE LOOKS INTO THE sky and lets loose a shout,
   questioning everything he had learned about.

   the thunder answers back,
   roaring loudly then leaving everything black.

   he stands there, alone again.
   wondering when this cycle will ever end.

   always tasting the temptation that travels with happiness,
   until it pulls away laughing in fits.

   he's left there by himself,
   keeping his darkest secret to none but self.

   what good is telling someone you're going to die,
   when all they would say is why?

he's alone with death,
taking a deep breath.

he looks into the sky once more,
his body physically and emotionally sore.

he closes his eyes,
watching as time flies.

DEPENDENCE

THE DEPENDENCE ON OTHERS to be content,
is life's greatest contempt.
we think we know what we need.

we strive to be the happiest we can,
yet sometimes we're left sinking in the sand.
our brow dripping with a lonesome sweat bead.

we think that we need company to last,
causing us to hide behind a mask.
we're trapped behind the desire to be freed.

be happy alone,
causing your dependence on others to be dethroned.
just follow this simple lead.

if you don't allow you to be happy with yourself,

what makes you think you can be happy with someone
else?
do this first, then proceed.

happiness alone,
causes life to throw you a bone.
that's all you must have to succeed.

THE HARVEST

I PLANT THE SEEDS,
 just to watch them grow,
 knowing 'i made that'.

 wishing for them to simply succeed.
 my own creations to show,
 to be better than i perhaps.

 their will i have freed,
 each planted in their own row.
 each picking up the others slack.

 i give them one warning, one plead.
 never give up, no matter the hardships you undergo.
 steer away from the pure black.

 i want them to grow strong,

to become beautiful beings.
live without dependence on me.

however, i know some will go wrong.
and the rest will suffer because of these few fiends.
then i will have to let them all see.

most will belong,
i will hear them as the rain pours down and they sing.
but not all will be free.

some will sing a dreary song.
and with that, the harvest they will bring.
that's just the way it must be.

to save them from falling from grace,
i must take them away.
bring them back home.

i'll bundle them up, their limpness is mine to embrace.
this is no place for them to stay,
beginning to creep out the garden and roam.

it's a sad reality i must face,
cutting them down, watching them pile up and fray.
nothing lasts forever without my throne.

it's a dream they all chase,
one i must slay.
watching the ones that become alone.

the stronger these plants get,
the more of a threat they become.
sadly, i cannot let that happen.

now, the harvest is when they seem fit.
these creations, i am where they came from.
their paths i had been mapping.

i knew before too long the end would hit.
i wanted to see them grow, i hate when the harvest must
come.
i watched them from the time they were a sapling.

they grow tall to end up in a pit,
most burning away, but replanting some.
to experience this again happening.

THE LONELY FARMER

WE ALL KNOW THE farmer,
   who watches from afar.
   he silently plants his crops,
   going about his business.

   he has a strict schedule, from which he doesn't deter.
   most of his work he does by the light of a star.
   always working, he never stops.
   listening to the innocents wishes.

   he plants the seed,
   watches it grow into a beautiful creation,
   watering it,
   building it up.

he protects it from the weed.
it's quite the dilemma he is facing,
when too soon it becomes fit,
the process of growing he has to disrupt.

he sees the beauty,
the innocence.
the youth.
the potential.

he has a job to do, regardless of what he may see.
the plant has grown too far up the fence,
he must take it down with a quick swoosh.
sometimes growing too fast can be consequential.

he pulls out his scythe,
and approaches the unknowing plant.
pulls the hood over his head,
and tears it down.

he shows little blithe,
as he is used to this transplant,
moving the plant from life to a silent bed.
he does it without a sound.

the plant had so much life left,
but the farmer had to do what he had to survive.
his pale complexion shining in the moonlight,
taking another plant from the ground.

this simple life, taken by theft.
what a surprise,
to see it taken without a fight.
perhaps the plant had a reason to frown.

LOADED

THREATENED WITH A LOADED gun,
  he does it for fun.

  finger on the trigger,
  eyes get bigger.

  face becomes lit,
  "go ahead, pull it"

  hammer goes back,
  the whole world gets black.

  he's going to get his wish,
  final offering in the dish

EXPANDED LOAD

HOW DO YOU THREATEN someone with a loaded gun,
   when they do it to them self for fun?

   as he slides his finger on the trigger,
   his victim's eyes get bigger.

   the innocent man's face becomes lit,
   as he shouts into his attacker's face, "go ahead and pull it"

   he pulls the hammer ever so slowly back,
   and the whole world washed away by a burning black.

   this is it, he's finally going to get his wish,
   this is it; he puts his final offering into the dish.

ALCOHOL

BOTTLE TO MY LIPS,
    alcohol sweeter than our last kiss,
    something i will always miss.

    alone i lay,
    thinking of how i've become this way,
    what a price i've been forced to pay.

    no other way to be,
    but the way everyone else can see.
    no way to be free.

BLACKNESS

I'M GOING TO DO great things,
    but why do i feel so lonesome?
    when i get to the top,
    what does it mean if i'm alone?

    while everyone else sings,
    i'm alone playing the drum.
    i listen as my heart begins to drop,
    like a falling stone.

    i'm destined for greatness,
    i'm destined for loneliness.

    i climb the tallest mountain,
    to stand atop its peak,
    only to look down,
    and see nobody cares about my success.

alone i am drowning,
i don't know what i truly seek.
in my reflection i see a frown,
even when i'm at my best.

all i see is a blackness,
all i see is a darkness.

SILENCE

MY SILENCE IS A savior,
  to save us from further misery.
  why can't you open your eyes to see?
  it's killing me to have this behavior.

  these actions aren't pain free,
  i oft feel like a failure,
  hiding from you in a small shelter.
  i know, this is how it must be.

  this life is full of danger,
  feelings being one, you may agree.
  one that you cannot flee.
  that leaves you with pent up anger.

  just shut up and breathe,
  this silence couldn't be faker,

please, someone just take her.
so my mind can finally be at ease...

SCARS

YOU CAN CALL OUT to the world,
   show them my scars,
   to hide your own.

   my cuts went down to the bone,
   straight and solid bars.
   my last lines crumpled.

   you are so quick to point out the error of my ways,
   when with dogs and ticks your own bed lays.
   a lie eventually frays.

   judge me for what i do,
   just make sure it's not something you do too.
   judgment is a bitter fruit.

PREACHER

FROM THE PREACHER AT my very own funeral,
   looks of dismay,
   as i sit by myself and pray.

i beg to stay,
but not knowing what else to say.
knowing that surviving isn't so crucial,
with my mind on the verge of removal.

stand up against the refusal,
take the beating no matter how brutal,
but do not become too fray,
as those you trust will eventually betray.

read into the gray,
between the black and white you are sent to lay,
as the darkness expands from your pupil,

it leaves your mind with thoughts so frugal.

you want to remain neutral,
but you know your mind and heart won't remain mutual.
your heart put up on display,
your mind continues with another parlay.
it plays over again like a shakespearean screenplay,
and you scream to stop the replay.
as the crowd shouts emanuel,
and drowns out your cries with another hymnal.

INTELLIGENCE

THEY SAY SMALL WRITING shows concentration,
   intelligence derived from the imagination.

   lack of sleep shows the mind constantly working,
   never stopping and always learning.

   talking to yourself stimulated the mind,
   helps you see what else you can find.

   signs of intelligence,
   coincide with a lack of sense.

   perhaps being so smart,
   is just the start.

REALITY

HAVE YOU EVER FELT like you cared too much,
  about those who never care enough?
  reality is tough.
  every person i met shows me such.

  i care about them all,
  but they could watch me fall.
  and not blink an eye at what they saw.
  not a one would stand in awe.

  to watch the people you care for push you away,
  is my simple minded fate.
  the thought causes my soul to dissipate,
  and fall away in life's dark lake.

  all i want is for someone to show me it's okay,
  to keep going this way.

that someday,
i won't be the only one to pray.

i'll have someone to pray for me,
without wanting something in return, just for free.
to chop down the family tree,
and build a boat for us to flee.

but alas, i fear this will never be the case,
as people smile to my face,
and stab me in the back with a warm embrace,
only to leave this bitter taste.

MR. MOON

THE MOON SHINES BRIGHT,
  at night.
  he shows his mighty might,
  his light.

  he hides during the day,
  they say.
  the sun wants to come out to play,
  she may.

  he is the protector of the weak,
  at his peak.
  in times of need they will always seek,
  his mystique.

  only in darkness do they see him shine,
  on their time.

never do they look for him when they're fine,
a lonely lifetime.

WRITERS

FALL IN LOVE WITH a writer,
  and you will never die.

  fall in love with a writer,
  he will give you all that he has.
  he gives you his heart,
  and that's just the start.

  fall in love with a writer,
  and he lets your soul fly.
  he immortalizes you with a pen stroke.
  your soul will never go broke.

  fall in love with a writer,
  he sees things not seen to the naked eye.
  the beauty beneath your skin,
  what truly matters in the end.

fall in love with a writer,
and he will never die.

FAMILY TREE

HERE I AM,
   from the family tree,
   hung.
   over and over again.
   cast to the tip,
   see what you have done?
   so much blood lost,
   it has me seeing double.
   this life wasted.
   "shit."
   faced with reality,
   i go back to being pijany.

LOVING

DO YOU CARE TO see what i have to offer?
  words spoken ever so softer.

  do you care to see my full potential?
  my love, my dear, is not circumstantial.

  do you care to feel loved by love itself?
  hidden away like fine liquor on the top shelf.

  oh how i do love thee,
  if only loving you were free.
  if only loving you did not involve three.
  if only loving you was not blind, but could see.
  oh how i do plea.

POETIC

POETIC TONGUE,
  like when the morning jay sung.

  old soul,
  glowing like burning coal.

  wise beyond the years,
  passing all my peers.

  eyes that speak,
  a language at its peak.

  now the jay dangles from the tree hung,
  the coal burns away in a hole,
  my peer's eyes fill with tears amongst their fears,
  at a language spoken only by a freak.
  the jay hangs with a broken beak,

blood falls forming flawed smears,
as the flame engulfs its bowl.
"what has this world brung",
the morning jay sung.

THE ASK

"IS THERE ANYTHING YOU need?"
   you ask me,
   just trying to be kind to me,
   even though you have so much on your hands.

   "yes."
   i tell you.
   know that you didn't want to hear that,
   knowing i've already made a mistake.

   "what is it?"
   silence.
   i want you to already know,
   what it is that i need.

   "nothing."
   i finally say,

telling you would be frivolous.
it wouldn't matter if you knew.

"you, you're all i need."
i whisper as you walk away,
begging you secretly to stay,
knowing it's best for you to that way.

BROKEN GLASS

HE'S CAUGHT LOOKING THROUGH a broken glass,
   reminiscent of a broken past.
   every shard a memory,
   of his life gone by too fast,
   gone in a flash.

   the light shines through with broken rays,
   pushing his mind into a haze,
   revealing what nobody else can see.
   kneeling in broken glass he prays,
   forgiveness for his troubled ways.

   as the glass presses beneath his leg,
   he sobs and continues to beg,
   only wanting to finally be free.
   does god hear every word he has said?
   does god see every scar that has bled?

COFFEE, ALCOHOL, AND HEARTBREAK

fingers intertwined with glass in between,
he lets out a blood curdling scream.
his prayer turns into a plea.
as the pain becomes all too keen,
the glass is no longer clean.
'just one more drink'
the lie i always think.
drinking to ease the pain,
to get away from the brink.
everytime it's the same,
drink until my body feels lame.

the alcohol touches the lip,
the stomach churns and feels sick.
but i keep going,
to ease the pain left by your last kiss.
the alcohol never stops flowing,
like the love for you i'm knowing.

'just a few more swallows'
i stutter as the alcohol follows.
as the world goes black,
my heart slowly hollows.
i call for you to come back,
but the door slams shut on the shack.

all that remains is your sweet taste,
and a distant memory of your beautiful face.
your memory slowly fades away,
but in my heart you will always have a place.

T.B. WITTKOFSKY

a love gone astray,
with a heart left as prey.

ONE NIGHT

IT WAS SUPPOSED TO be one night,
   a drunken desire.
   i left without a word,
   little did i know it would turn into a fight.

   i'm awoken, tired.
   your drunken words were all i heard.
   "we don't speak after this night ends."
   words burning like a fire.

   out of two, i came in third.
   we started off as friends,
   but we let the alcohol fuel our desire.
   little did i know what would be offered.

I'M TRYING

WHAT IF I TOLD you i'm trying?
   i'm doing my best to keep on going.
   slowly, i'm dying.

   what if i told you i'm giving it my all?
   slowly, my blood is flowing.
   i just feel like i always fall.

   what if i told you this is my best?
   i never claimed to be all knowing,
   but you know the rest.

   what if i told you it's all for you?
   as my love is slowly growing.
   i want you to want me too.

COFFIN

YOUR NAME ETCHED INTO my coffin,
    like when it was scarred on my skin.
    the pallbearers slowly carry my casket,
    secretly wanting to blow away my ashes.

    taking sips from their flasks,
    there's a since of apathy from the masses.
    the smell of misery blows with the wind,
    and the silence of disappointed sin.

    it's a sweet kiss given to all men,
    a small prick by a pin.
    the preacher uses her last breath,
    to speak to all who are left.

    as the people pray for my death,
    my body's slowly undressed.

my body lies,
atop a sea of cold lies.

as if my life wasn't pain enough,
life after proves to be even more tough.

ı WONDER

I WONDER.
   where will i be,
   in a lustrum?

   i wonder.
   who will i be,
   in a decade?

   i wonder.
   what will my memory be,
   in a century?

   i wonder.
   will i make it,
   until tomorrow?

PRODIGAL SON

I'VE LIVED MY LIFE with closed eyes,
   strung along by lies.
   what are family ties?
   arent ties meant to come undone?

   you can call me the prodigal son,
   but all i see is a burnt out sun.
   such a bitter tongue.
   they say blood is thicker than water.

   i can drown in water, for a starter.
   i'll trade you my blood in a barter,
   i bet mine boils when it's hotter.
   they've tied a noose from the family tree.

   i guess they're going to hang me,
   even with closed eyes that's not hard to see.

that's when i wonder where is he?
stand alone by my side.

CELESTIAL

DEATH IS IMMINENT,
 that doesn't make it any less hell bent.
 like a message god sent,
 to take you from the covenant.

DEATH'S DEALER

AS MY MIND FADES,
nobody sees it in my face.
the dealer deals,
and all i get is spades.

i realize this isn't my place,
how the hell did i get here?
i'm on eleven,
the only card i need is a face.

in everyone's eyes shines fear,
but it's too late for that,
i'm too far ahead,
i call my bluff for the dealer to hear.

the dealer and i made a pact,
he'd hit me with an ace,

and i'd play out the rest.
the decisive dealer took his word back.

LOVE. HATE.

IT'S AS IF THEIR eyes glazed over their own holes,
 filling in where the alcohol missed.
 this world, confused, circles the moon.
 two best friends talking in a lover's tongue.
 confused eyes gaze at the stars as they dance in the dark,
 drunk on the idea of four letter words,
 love. hate.

SENSES

BREATHE IN THE SCENT of my love,
    and let it fill your lungs.
    let my radiant love rays,
    beat down on your skin with its healing ways.
    look into my caring eyes,
    and let them break your broken ties.
    listen to the love in my voice,
    realize you and i are the final choice.
    i still hope that in the end,
    it will be you and i that fade away in the wind.

TOMORROW

LIVE LIKE TOMORROW IS your last day,
because there is no tomorrow.
when tomorrow gets here,
it's today.
live in the day,
because it could be your last.
nothing lasts forever,
except death.

LIES

LIES TOLD FROM THE lips of an angel,
   overly confident in their life decisions.
   venomous words sprayed gently,
   enveloping the truth it shrouds.
   in a dark night,
   silence is the loudest sound.
   even demons laugh,
   vehemently at lost lovers;
   implying that they're saints in disguise.
   lost lovers laugh loudly and loosely.

you

EVERY SECOND THAT PASSES by,
every memory i make with you,
all makes me crave your love even more.

i see your hair blow on the beach,
your eyes sparkle in the moon light,
and i yearn for your love more than before.

i watch you as you laugh about our silly conversations,
i listen to you silently sing to the radio,
and i fall even more into love.

i see the distress in your face when you look at me,
and think of your boyfriend,
as you realize you're not in love with him.

the pain that hits me when you go to his arms,

the emptiness that i feel when you're gone,
my heart aches from being so big.

SECRETS

A HUNDRED MILES AWAY,
    i still smell your scent.
    i reach my hand out,
    in hopes you'll grab it,
    through the shadows of forbidden love.

    secrets held by a thousand dove.
    our words intertwine into a perfect fit,
    if only they could hear our silent shout.
    only you knew what i meant,
    when i couldn't figure out what to say.

    a single person stands in our way,
    showing you where the wrongs went,
    planting that sorry seed of doubt.
    filling in the darkness of our loves pit.
    down we fall with a shallow shove.

your past and future loves,
two in the same.
sadly, your present,
is one difference not easily overlooked.

WINDY

THE WIND WHISPERS WHIMPERS from afar,
    turning the ice in my veins into blood.
    two lovers crossed by a shooting star,
    as the world disappears into a red flood.

    the nighttime air picks up where you left off,
    chilling my goose bumps into chicken pox.
    the type of love that causes even the devil to scoff,
    lifting up the world on building blocks.

    angels cry gruesome tears,
    as i walk alone through a storm of emotion,
    a storm that's failed to cease for years.
    causing an overflow from the apathetic ocean.

    as i drown in a sea of desire,
    i reach for the life jacket you throw to save me,

only to find it made of bricks from the hands of a liar.
i drown to finally be free.

NOW

DO I KNOW YOU?

are you the one i shared a simple kiss with?
the kiss that made my body go numb,
and made me feel invincible?

do i know you?
are you the one i shared drinks with?
until we started to stammer,
and then decided just one more wouldn't hurt.

do i know you?
are you the one i stayed up with until wee hours of the
morning?
letting go of my secrets,
only to hold onto yours.

do i know you?

are you the one who's hand fit perfectly into mine?
who's touch gave my goosebumps,
and heated the ice chest in my chest?

do i know you?
are you the one who i shared all these memories with?
are you the one who i made a million more with?
are you the one who got away?

do i know you?
a million things pass through my mind,
only one thing sticks out:
i used to.

SINGLE

ALONE,
  i'm here
  inevitably.

  people come
  and
  people go.

  fast
  and
  slow.

  they all leave,
  some
  will stay longer.

  i made it

this far
with just myself.

i can make it,
the rest of the way,
alone.

LOSER

I'M LOSING SLEEP,
   losing friends,
   losing focus,
   losing my mind,
   losing myself,
   losing my life.

WHITE PILL

A WORLD CONTROLLED BY a white pill,
   that tells you how to feel.
   the men in white coats,
   give you false hopes.

INCENSE

SHE LOST HER INNOCENCE to the smell of bad incense.
  her choices led by the voices in her head,
  the ones that tell her she's a failure.

  in one quick breath he made her sick,
  the smell of suffering and hell.
  he whispers to her and she feels the brush of his whiskers.

  it's as if she knew the things he said could never be,
  but still she held onto things she wished to feel.
  only he knew the truth of how she flew.

SLUMBER

IF IN MY SLEEP,
    i were to die tonight,
    how would you remember me?
    for have i made an impact,
    and touched your life?
    or would i be forgotten,
    and my memory turned to dust?

COFFEE, ALCOHOL, HEARTBREAK

COFFEE,
  alcohol,
  heartbreak.

  that's all it will take,
  watch a great man fall,
  watch him turn into me.

  kept awake,
  just long enough to make,
  the happiness not feel so fake.

  life goes blurry,
  because everyone is in such a hurry,

to be in such a worry.

sorrow sets in.
as the three blend,
and the world begins...

RACE

WHY IS IT SO hard,
for humankind,
to be kind?
like we're all trying to get far,
in some sort of race,
against the humanrace.

MY CONCLUSION

WHAT BETTER ENDING,
  to a beginning,
  than a conclusion,
  drawn from collusion.

INSIDE THE MIND

LOOK INTO MY MIND.
what do you see?
it should be you.

thinking of you,
i let my mind fly,
and my soul unwind.

it's amazing what a lost soul can find,
in a simple pass by,
when i came across you.

i feel as if i should thank you,
and i know you're wondering 'why?'
i can see now that i'm not blind.

it was the way your eyes shined,

when you looked at this simple guy,
and all he could do was look at you.

he couldn't look away from you,
the look of want and need that shone from his eye,
it was one of a kind.
a match that god designed,
as he flew into the sky,
he was given the gift of you.

SEASHORE

A SOUL LOST AT sea,
   with eyes that couldn't see.

   washed upon the shore,
   where he wasn't sure.

FEATURED

EYES SO WISE,
   that tell a thousand different stories.
   they reveal a new truth,
   with each longing glance.

   a smile that hangs like the moon,
   shines bright in a dreary night.
   innocence peaks through,
   and steals away my breath.

   radiant beauty,
   illuminates an entire lifetime.
   i feel you steal my mind,
   for a moment and a half.

   i can hear your voice,
   soothing to the soul,

stopped my heart,
because i sought what i thought was an angel.

EMPTY

THE END OF A cigarette,
   burning red,
   shrinking down with every breath.

   the bottle of alcohol,
   tipped up,
   draining in between gulps of air.

   the ember falls to the ground,
   the last drop is emptied,
   and the last breath is breathed.

THE ESCAPE

WHEN YOUR OWN MIND scares you,
how do you escape it?
it's something you created,
but your biggest regret.
your escapes are temporary-
recess time on the schoolyard.
the alcohol brings you to a distant state of mind,
the drugs take you to a new life.
but it's all temporary.
all of it except your mind.
even when you die,
your mind remains.
to haunt you through the depths of hell.

BREATHING TECHNIQUES

JUST KEEP BREATHING;
   take one breath at a time.
   have some sort of feeling,
   tell yourself you'll be fine.

   in.
   out.

WAVERIDER

WAVES CRASH DOWN,
washing away all that was built.
in a darkness,
a sliver of light beats down,
only to be seen covered by a single cloud.
leaving an expansive darkness,
that swallows everything it touches.
all that floats on top,
is seen engulfed by crashing waves.
the longer you stare across the darkness,
the less you can see.
eventually,
it seems more appealing,
to be swallowed by that darkness,
than to watch it,
and wait for another glimmer of light.

PASS

THIS, TOO, SHALL PASS.
  just not fast enough.
  maybe life is rough now,
  but don't throw in the towel yet.

NEVER THE SAME

A RELIT CIGARETTE,
   never taste the same.
   the musty taste sets,
   as smoke fades from a rekindled flame.

   an open bottle of liquor,
   will not taste the same,
   it could make your stomach twist and sicker,
   then you look for whom to blame.

   a bottle of pills once used,
   won't taste the same.
   as the pills become infused,
   turning your insides into what you became.

   you can t take something you once loved,
   and expect it to be the same.

when pushed and shoved,
it's an impossible feeling to reclaim.

ONCE UPON A TIME

WHAT YOU ONCE WERE,
   you are no longer.

   who i once was,
   i am now stronger

   what we once were,
   has become a goner.

   when a 'friend'.
   has no more favors to ask,
   the light will shine and bend,
   with what has passed.

   friends come and go,
   family stays forever,
   blood or otherwise, oh,

the ties do sever.

THE VOW

HOW TIMES HAVE CHANGED,
    for better or worse.
    the vows of the past,
    come full circle.

    the words once hurtful,
    cut through at last.
    when the thoughts become averse,
    the heart becomes manged.

    from the family tree he hanged,
    until the blood cells do burst,
    at the final mass,
    calling on the faithful.

    the baby rocking in a cradle,
    with the wind oh so fast,

taking a long ride in a hearse,
hearing the voice harangue.

the sound of emptiness rang,
the family getting terse.
what once was a loud blast,
now swings silently on a cable.

LESSONS LEARNED

CLAIM WHAT YOU ONCE lost,
with the passion you sought.
life lessons taught,
leave you with naught.

and to reach for the stars,
is to forget the scars,
left by prison bars.

letting go of the past,
to ensure it's your last.

regain what is rightfully yours.

OKAY

I'M NOT OKAY,
   all i want to say -
   how do i say,
   when i don't know what to say?

CONTROL

ANGRY AND OUT OF control,
   slipping through life's folds,
   escaping my own hold.

   hearing the cries of the innocent,
   and those hellbent,
   dirty as flint.

   the angels cry louder,
   for those who lack power,
   than those who hold the powder.

LISTEN

SPEAKING SILENT SECRETS,
    serenading swan songs,
    someone swims solo.

    thundering ticking,
    tocking together thoroughly,
    tightening the temptations.

    liars listening loosely,
    lives laying lightly,
    lying lights let live.

    with whispers whispering,
    wondering who was where,
    why we would waste wonders.

    breaking bleakly beneath both,

batting bloodshots blatantly,
bathing between bloomings.

About the Author

T.B. Wittkofsky is a storyteller, educator, and community builder who uses his personal experiences to help others rise with their stories. With a background in marketing, communications, and mental health advocacy, his work blends strategy with heart. T.B. has taught courses on branding, social media, and entrepreneurship, guiding students and creatives through the evolving digital landscape.

After overcoming challenges like addiction, job loss, and financial instability, T.B. embraced a life on the road in an RV with his wife and three dogs, finding clarity, healing, and inspiration in the journey. He now leads Adventure with Coffee, a blog and podcast that celebrates connection through culture, travel, and, of course, coffee.

As the former president of the North Brunswick Chamber of Commerce and founder of Tea With Coffee Media, T.B. has helped countless entrepreneurs and small businesses find their voice. His advocacy work, including panels on mental health and representation in fiction, underscores his mission to create safe, inclusive spaces for honest storytelling.

Whether mentoring writers, consulting on marketing campaigns, or writing stories that reflect lived truths, T.B. shows up with compassion, curiosity, and an unwavering belief in the power of the narrative.

Other Works

(Not) Alone
A Mental Health Novella

Salt Lines:
A Poetry Collection

The Principal's Principles
Literary Fiction Based on a True Story

The Sunflower Kisses Series
A Man's POV Romance

T.B. WITTKOFSKY

Book 1: The Seeds of Love

<u>Enamored Echoes (with Kelsey Anne Lovelady)</u>
Romantic Fantasy Series

Book 1: Potent

www.ingramcontent.com/pod-product-compliance
Lightning Source LLC
Chambersburg PA
CBHW021203130626
46554CB00005B/1961